I0527952

The Somatoliths
Copyright © 2024 James Cole

Original Cover Art by Gnashing Teeth Publishing

The fonts used are Amasis MT Bold Black and Times New Roman
The cover font is IM FELL French Canon

All rights reserved. No duplication or reuse of any selection is allowed without the express written consent of the publisher.

Gnashing Teeth Publishing
242 East Main Street
Norman AR 71960
http://GnashingTeethPublishing.com

Printed in the United States of America

ISBN 979-8-9898345-6-3

Library of Congress Control Number: 2024931106

Non-Fiction: Poetry

Gnashing Teeth Publishing First Edition

The Somatoliths
by
James Cole

In medieval science the fundamental concept was that of certain sympathies, antipathies, and strivings inherent in the matter itself. Everything has its right place, its home, the region that suits it, and, if not forcibly restrained moves thither by a sort of homing instinct, a "kindly enclyning" to their "kindly stede."

- C.S. Lewis, *The Discarded Image*

On Stones

I suppose anything so old is owed a discussion of origin.

A stone is quintessentially a solid thing but ultimately, every spike of obsidian or nub of gravel derives from something superheated, liquid, churned up, spat out, cooled, stratified, buried, unburied. The exact processes do not lend themselves to human understanding. We don't have the patience for them, only the utility.

A stone is only discernible from its particulates if concreted to scale with metrics of the naked eye. Anything less is dust. Anything more is a mountain. Anything undecided goes without saying because it's humans making these decisions.

I'm making the decision, now, aren't I? With what is stone being stone, and what is flesh being flesh, and all else is agreement of the two. I'm not so willing to admit I have a will.

It is quite unlike a stone to think these things.

The Gastrolith

The Gastrolith

I want to talk about a particular stone from my childhood. It came to me in those liminal, ante-adolescent years, when I was still a fixture at my local science museum. There they kept a geological exhibit outlining every period from Precambria to our current Quarternary mess. The Jurassic placard included a touchable specimen, something excavated from a sauropod's ribcage, a relic that would not look out of place among the decorative stones spread between serenely stationed topiary.

Gastrolith. Stomach stone. Greek sounded less ancient to me back then. These masses were swallowed and are still swallowed to this day by reptiles, birds, I think some seals. From massive tumblers to shredding gravel, these inorganic chunks are retained in the digestive system to aid in the breakdown of foodstuffs, though they are themselves, indigestible.

As toddlers we are told not to put things in our mouths. As a toddler, I'm sure I would've tried to swallow that museum stone were it not glued down. According to my childhood mind, such things were better suited to my insides than to a cold exterior. But I had teeth. I could chew. What then, I wonder, needed processing? I have a sense of that need now. It doesn't have a name or an exact shape, and it doesn't pass without aid.

They tore down that exhibit. I remember feeling hurt that I wasn't consulted on its recycling. Ten-year-old me took a lot of things personally.

I've since drifted from the paleontological, though stones still float as an aspect of obsession. And in the years since I lost that gastrolith, I've discovered many other bodily rocks. Body and rocks—those two don't seem like they should mix and yet we keep finding one inside the other.

Some are taken, some are made, either way it's tiresome carrying all these stones. I'd be better suited waiting for their effect. And though I tend toward obedience, I'm trying to fight my inclinations. I'm told this is how shit gets done.

Thank God for my Esophagus

Thank God for my esophagus, this bit of potted air, my snake,
my face so full of itself, I chase its peristalsis like a frisbee
forcing air, and yes, I'm told the best toys are those that
call it quits in the esophagus, thank God I am all grown up,
thank God the rest is invested in stocks of bone, thank God I will
be broth one day, when I shall indeed be what I eat, and holy, holy, holy
shall be the sound in my esophagus

Thank God for being something, for oozings and spare modes
of breath, thank God for anal breathing and all it's done for pigs,
and thank God for all we've done to pigs, sausage so fit for our
esophagus, thank God for the Heimlich, in flaps and fans and our
totally on brand in being human, thank God for this epiglottis,
even if doesn't always close just right, even if it loses the trachea
on occasion, thank God for its invasion

Thank God for all accessories, my upgrades and unfaded foppish
curl, thank God for its lacerations and its healing with gauze,
thank God for my never having a massage, its ease too opposed
to knotting, thank God for nodding, how flexible it makes
the esophagus, and thank God for being a river, a fen, hardline
against worrisome mists but then again thank God for all
the worry, the road in profile

Thank God for being half a person in textbooks and charts,
my dissection always another disagreement, it isn't
too hard to imagine when you've got all this esophagus,
thank God for all of us, thank God for their not being a God,
especially one with an esophagus, thank God for stretch,
its odd moments measured in its flexion, its enchiridion
of closed, conflustered space

Thank God for sounding hollow, median meat so dense
around me I could never be well done, and thank God
for doing well,   I mean, we get away with it sometimes,
like a crank and its bucket, thank God for clean water,
an altar of cycles, this idyll of cooling in the esophagus,
thank God for cooling and drooling out of mouths and palates—
all awful auctions of the esophagus

thank God for thinking in thirds, the worst less because of it,
the worst cases being what they will and power foaming over
in thankful clots of the esophagus, thank God for being thankful,
thank God it sounds like this, goes like swift kindle flaking white
and downy, there's nothing so brutal as change, thank God
for fame eating its own esophagus, for being as easy as it looks,
it is easy anyway, sometimes I can even speak.

eat right

You may be tempted to say something like:
    you don't eat right
and I may be tempted to respond with:
    I don't eat period
but let's face it, we won't say either
because we're too goddamn
polite and thin

A dollar in change

I think it all started when
my parents told me to save money
in an IRA. I was listening to "Sabotage"
by the Beastie Boys at the time. All I could think was:
Why should I be giving money to Irish irredentists?
And I haven't been to a dentist in a while, I should go,
I have the insurance. There was that terrible sore
but it went away fine, though I still bleed out my gums.
It's money in my pocket that I don't have, like that
dollar in change I used to carry until I gave it
to a desperate man because I couldn't ignore
or pretend again. It's just alright kid, you'll do
what you feel is best and regret its lessness later.
But it's a little more than scripture, a little more
than truancy. I gave up those quarters because
they were there to be given, presence precedes
and follows absence, except when it comes to ourselves
with ourselves. I bet he thought that too, hands heavy
with change, thinking healthy things, like how someday
I'll miss today or how others might wonder when
and why I started funding resistance armies and I'll tell them:
every person's got a right to their own country.
And then I turned into the 7-11 and tried not to think
about all those fucking nail bombs.

Summer Camp

We'll see who remembers their limbs
when, breaching back into breath, we stand naked,
see the summer roar from our mountain lake

I will erupt from the depths, gripping either
gill of the muddy king who makes waterpunk
with air-starved slaps of his forked-fin tail

As he asphyxiates, we will mirth raucous,
pass his final throes from arm to arm, let his
mail shimmer coat our slimeless mammal skins

Then come mouthfuls, our call to communion,
solely swooned in show of season, jaws poised,
indulgent, inevitable, just bite it, it's edible

By the time the spine is shown we grow
too sick to fuck, and surely, in these shallows
none feel younger than a thousand years

Birthday Suit

There's something rearranged in me,
the heart of this, my artery
distracts the head, and if I sneeze,
squeeze out the parts I hardly need.

Since when was I a blood collage,
appeasement in this flesh garage,
enmeshed in what is best for love,
or, lacking that, the lack thereof?

No good the gut too flushed to churn,
or eyes comprised of veiny burn,
no good the hands, no good the feet,
no good this abacus of meat.

And I, the calculating grasp
deflated voice with faulty rasp
that bears no sound and yet is heard
in punctured passings of a word.

And what a load of *yikes* to think
of anything with all this pink,
gelatinized, but I still wish
the rest is bronze and knows no squish.

Yesterday I realized I was following someone, and I didn't know why

We see it in nature too—
army ants shoveling a death spiral
in cement, the most hurried waiting
to exist in invertebrates
                                    but that's
nothing before our own following
of the asses right in front of us
like junkie clockwork processing
before a great black rock,
or careless crumb, in the case
of ants, honoring that which they
cannot seem to eat, and, even now,
it seems to me that all images
destroy themselves in time.

and turtles use the moon

I don't trust people   because
I know them   or   I don't know them

they are, in some reports, no more than a lozenge
of lonely lopers, caustic alchemies in artisan remorse,
lumpy homunculi possessed by a trio of ghosts,
one controlling the legs but whining that it would rather
lever the arms, another massaging heart and lungs
into function, never kneading a breath, the last not
wanting to be inside a human at all.

We should have possessed a turtle it says
at least then we can close up shop
        on occasion.
At least then I may shut my eyes,
        peer through nostrils,
        not worry about
        the missing scrunch of jigsaw.
        Turtles, I hear,
        are famously unable to shrug.

Eating Out

yesterday,
I was looking small
like limpen leftovers in
a St. Bernard's-worth of doggy bag,
my consumers wondering why
they brought me home at all, thinking:
we could've finished it there,
we weren't that full.

And I wonder what is worse
the creature that can fit you
in its mouth entire
or the one that can't
but does so anyway,
piece by patient piece.

Pectoralis Major

I was asked, mid-rolling of my arms,
what hurt and I, knowing I should
always be specific in what hurts me,
answered: *why, my pectoralis major*

And when the panhandler called me
a *whippy motherfucker* I asked him
his name
          Albert, he said, staring
suddenly at himself, because I
should also know the names of
what tries to hurt me, even if it
doesn't sting to its fullest fancy,
even if, I'm sorry to say, I can't
feel it through some other muscle

I don't think it has much to do with
lactic acid anymore, but could I
use each injury in a sentence?
Could they be spelled, dispelled,
protracted in the learning of their names?

The other day I almost choked
to death on an unknown morsel,
yellow in its serving.
          I survived,
but hunched forward, found no name
for the obstruction, thought so
literally little of it, but still cried myself
out of paying the bill

The Post-Oneiric Breakfast Debacle

I ruined Grandad's high-blood-pressure socks
with cereal milk.   "What were you doing
                        eating cereal in *my* socks?"
                        he asked.

"It couldn't be helped,"
I said. "I miss the sugar
rushes I could cram down
as a child. Now, it's all
headaches, and sag, and
remembering that you
are dead, and that all I
could do was stare up
at the ceiling when they
found you on your back.
You had just seen the
doctor the week before."

                        "Doc says I'll live until
                        ninety-seven."
"I might've become
myself by then, not a
foraging cartoon echo.
We would have had
time then to disagree,
resent the worlds we
came from. I would've
thought more of your
choice of radish words,
your drill sergeantry."

                        "When I was your age."
"When I was my age,
I thought you knew

the clot was coming,
you had the socks
to prepare. Now all
I have is this cereal,
and your circulation,
and the nightmares
that started a month
after we buried you:
you standing, specter
arm around me, your
parents' farm in our
beholding. I wasn't
scared that you were
alive in my dreams,
but that I would
wake and find you
only speaking
in a poem."

Fossil

Not knowing what to say to anyone ever, a sauropod
swallowed a stone so as to always have a conversation
starter, but, in doing so, disengaged an entire intestine's
worth of work, felt heavy, uncurled casual like the sea.

And, not knowing that speech had yet to be invented,
he lumbered to other herds and thundered in diplodicid
dialect, as if to say: *you know, there's a stone in my guts*,
then reconsidered, tried to pass, felt full for the first time.

He must've told someone because damn near everyone
is doing it these days. And by everyone, I mean anyone
with a touch of *out-of-touchness*: some punished birds,
those pardoned seals, our mineral ribs, and, well, me.

I found his carbon copy in the earth; cut and chiseled
the bedrock spare. Took the weathered stone and glued
it to a placard for a younger me to see. What I wrote
beneath took centuries to revise, rewrite, receive:

You never seemed so simple. So, why not be a stone
with its thousand parts compressed? You never seemed
so convoluted. Why not be a stone, a bludgeon of two
birds? You have only ever been a stone or a stone.

And, not knowing what to say to myself ever, I broke
it's flaking anchor, and took it, not to swallow, but to
stare, beveled symphony of fleet, forgotten tongues.
Knowledge deeper than a language can ever truly show.

Weighted questions of: *do you know what a miracle is?*
Would you recognize its flicker if you saw it mellowed
in a borrowed shade of blue? A careening cut of red?
Would you call it stone, a piece of bread neither, both?

Knowing not to say anything, a stone returns to earth,
lest its absence be felt, a stomach which stomachs and
stones their only means to cope—in rivers, on split crags,
indigestible, everywhere, and free of human stay.

The Bufonite

Intermission

Popcorn at an 800% markup. A soda fountain with little to no remaining syrup. Sour Punch Straws which make everything taste like sour punch. Chocolate somethings which also taste too much of that American acid. The carpet is too scuffed and fraught with dust sprites. An usher is trying to surreptitiously study for his ACT in the corner coat room.

If you treat this like a play, someone is bound to comment on performances. If you're reading this, I guess that means you. The critics are harsh, but I want you to know you are doing a great job. You can stress the details of each line, try not to hoist yourself too high on any incendiary, get away unscathed. The promise is something you make to yourself. Only you can settle on its keeping.

If you treat this like a movie, wonder aloud what sort of movie puts its intermission this early in its runtime. Would you call poetry a thriller? A comedy? How many samurai have you counted? Have you formed your opinion on the shot composition? And who is commenting on who, what is ripping off what?

If you treat this like a magic show, pay no heed to the creatures that come slinking out my pant leg. They are incidental. The act itself is more a revision than a genuine trick. Like a case of curious surgery.

If you treat this like a surgery, then remember the toad. Limbs pinned into wax, formaldehyde a ruling scent. Everything prickles. From the membranes of a skull unseamed, we see a gem, born more of magic impetus than any medical means. Suddenly, science is no longer a science, and luck is no longer a radian on The Wheel, and a hum grows out of the great sacrifice: of egg becoming larvae becoming toad becoming bufonite. Deader now than dreaming, you too become an actor from a foreclosed odeon. Shit—who supplies these dissections?

The lights are dimming. Crowds murmur in procession, collapsing back to their seats. The usher waves the people down the aisles. He's done studying for tonight. He'll be ready come May.

For the Amphibian with the Crabgrass Wig

Cynthia Toadswoman
was to be married in the black mulch
when she realized: *yes, i can do more,*
and yes, i am more than warts, and yes,
that's a myth anyway, and yes, i will go
to the far side of the asphalt, and yes,
it is alright to eat bugs at every meal

Urodela

she who is emerging,
shardless thing of footprints
which towers at heights *higher than*
flexes accretion in feats primeval
wriggled free of loamy bed—
mightier than willing,
deadlier than done
her venom suppressed until
all atoned moments
demist, dripped glass affixed
in clear caress
but too easily the feeling
severed, first numb, tilted
then knowing swift partition
a three-legged scuttle
familiar limb gone,
and with it the net of nerves
felt and feeling, elicit,
spent, potential—
like a salamander removed

Simply put,

the mind is a fine place for crucifixion
the wax plate fair for a rood, rainwater
chamomile and polyester armor for my
long crusade in the rain, two miles until
my imminent Outremer comes spitting
through the streak. Some might say
that walking all this way, a company to
downpour, all for want of umbrella is,
simply put: *another game the martyr*
                          should not play

from home I have wandered, but for whom
have I squandered these partial astrides,
these carols of sibilant dawn, these rituals
of self becoming something else? Something
so willingly estranged, a wasp without its
hive, an eye in a mouth, so solemnly incensed
by color, sight, anything that tears and builds,
tears and gilds itself in edible foils, folly
freezing on unbreathing skin

The Antediluvian

I might smile a while
and while I'm smiling change—
I might age or add those
well-adjusted shades, colors
of a chameleon that defile
an erstwhile edge

Do you know
the way we count our days,
debates and disputations
on the human subject?

Did Noah in his
long life after The Flood
drink far too well,
take up the token nakedness?

He did not deliberate death
      but he did die deliberating

a lonely hotel courtyard in the middle of Atlanta

This pond is going green
and I don't mean in an ecological sense
or, I do, but sometimes
the figurative envy of water is tired code
for an oxygen sap,
      water struggles,
      things die

I look on and am surprised to see
tadpoles squiggle like fat little black
spermatozoa poaching at ripples,
nibbling, I think, at that liquid ruin
      and I am reminded of the aquarium
we used, for a desperate period, in kindergarten

our tadpoles more like shiny, whip-tailed olives
and the slow horror of the class
      as we processed, week by week,
that these dappled creatures were not
turning into frogs
      but something long

and lizard-like, less stoic mushroom caps
      bloated in the mud
more squirming, regenerative things,
that flattened their bellies daily
keening against the glass
      and now,

now I know why, with their water so green—
      green, but not in the ecological sense
      but also in the ecological sense
when my teacher called my parents and told them
I was "distracted, wandering off to other classes,"

        I didn't have the words at the time
to tell them about the green water,
the bare white bellies,
        the glass that was there
and the glass that wasn't,
        I was young
        I was much too young

The Summer Project
or The Cul-de-sac Mithraeum

Make like Mithras and cut the bull.
I've seen what synchronization
twists in a lunch of loose skin
like you.

Don't pretend with me. Those tools
in your hands are real, that hacksaw—real,
that wrench set—real, that fishing rod—
shall I say it?

If you want to build your temple
in a tree, don't ask me. You ask
the oak and hope it doesn't owe
the Board.

And if you want to take me
to your solar banquet then invictify
your right hand, hold it firm,
let me grasp and shake.

Sit a moment. Drink this.
No, I promise it is sugarless.
I know you like it sour, I know
the dinner call.

Isn't it too warm for a hat
like that? Take it off. I promise
I won't laugh—sorry. I really
thought I wouldn't.

Where will the altar go?
And the censers? The spelaeum?
How do you imagine the universe
so far from the ground?

This is nice. The glib slip gives
our white fence pretense a chance
to find its cloven footing. Bray
once for yes.

And when you sweat through,
swell with callous, slow your hands
and slouch, you can cut the bull,
come back inside. Hello.

The Loiter You Do

is the loiter you get.
What remains when we've loitered so long?
Is it spice from the fever, squall from the ether,
talk like we've never been wrong?

The loiter I have is the loiter I sold, the loiter
which bought this whole town. And the gist
is exactly the gist I remember the day the dark
loitered on down.

Through covens and bypass, the still will remember
like silence which smothers in song.
Then what will you do with the loiter you offer,
when the loiter gets loitered too long?

Caryatid

Be free, or be   a caryatid,
weight held   on the head.
Where others see a pillar
I see sward Arcadia and a
peninsular   pain,
cranial rock and for-
thcoming if. Then I tell
you to pose a little lon-
ger and you   break wei-
ght from firm to
contrapposto, chip-
ped entablature creas-
ing the marble neck. And
I bet it hurts, Love, like any
labor thrown lower
than your   lowest rib.
Like anything
erected with
legacy in mind.
Like, forgive me,
time is not
mine to mete
out. See?
I do
listen
some-
times.

The Wide White Gazebo

for Chebet

Out in waist-high weeds, the Wide White Gazebo
keeps insect courts and scratch-love dictations
in octagon. Where a voiding breeze might stir the trees'
disintegration, cover yet another year in the forest's shedding sleep.
Here, nothing is without context.

I don't know what IR + MA equals, but its formula
scrawls one column at least twelve seasons over. The oldest
iteration recedes mossy deep, and later refrains climb well around
a length of wood in shrinking parts. Parts—not one.
And the moth cocoons dress them.

Winter will erase nothing, it quilts and shies,
leans on the dormancy of others, or buries,
threatens to bite and shake a watcher blind. It will
come, and with fire we will fight it, as if
a creature from heaven's helm.

Some say only the living can fill themselves,
turn a field to famine, but anything untied,
unwritten, damned or smitten can taste
of wasted time. See them given up, dissolved,
see where silence is not still.

A green bug, with catching claws, copulates
then feasts its lover headless. A far cry from IR
or MA, whoever renews that yearly arithmetic.
They think of the love long after, real or not.
Who does the mantis pray to?

The Stationery Enabler

If you feel a lightness in the head,
whether by incense or gasoline,
and the air still feels too empty,
even in your lungs, even in strung up silence,
know that I will always send you matches.

Not that matches are all that
hard to get. Our world is overgrown
with phosphorus, narrow frictions,
provident plenties of books
and the makers of books.

It is an unwise habit, I'll admit,
this mass mailing of starters, like departure
from an atmosphere too green,
metalloluminescence
blunderbussing down en masse.

Can I show my contrail and still
be your type of person when I enter a room
and refuse to turn on the light?
Can I be so presently afar?
Can I really do no harm?

noonfall

I am one in my humanity,
you are two in yours
Conjoined, our trinity drips
hot like holy oil, three in heaven,
three in hell, burning slip
through basket gaps, tears
in a wicker bed that scald
our spun materials

Soaked by and soiled,
we wring ourselves, inner moisture
wrought for the world roots
Do you hear it groan its epoch?
Do you see its autumn taking
turn, bowing with progeny?
I would love you in this tree
I would love to see these forests
nourished by our drain

An acorn cracks, inside: another
acorn, unaccustomed noonfall
splitting bodies on a stone, the uproot
truth of you—other innards
peering through cracks of twice
tilled provision, the tragic wan
of sick and wasted succor

You either stay awake, or wait,
bedreamed, eaten by your expectation
And I might call it something beautiful
and you could call me 'poet'
and I'll shrink because while
some can name, and some can praise,
I think only of the way you breathe
in mountain shadow, and forgive me,
but there are no names for that

The Regurgitalith

Invocation

Spirits of the sloped, benighted air.

PRESTIGIAR, GROBIAN, PUCA, LOGOI, EUTHYPHRO

Who pass and are passed in the anointed chiasm. Gather in your shrink and pace. Step with agility from sidewalk square to sidewalk square, never touching the squiggled, sun-smote remains of earthworms expired black in sun.

As the magus manipulates symbols so must the poet manipulate symbols. As the scientist manipulates variables so must the poet manipulate variables. As the stone manipulates the stomach so must the poet manipulate the stomach.

KLEIN, MOBIUS, SIERPINKSI, KOCH, MANDELBROT

What good is a container if it cannot also spill? What good is the vessel if it itself is not finite? What good is good if it does not exist opposite to evil?

I conjure then, the wretch and roil, the filament upset, untangled from insides. I abjure the antinausea, the bilious flux, the futile fricatives of fullness' true fit. I opine for expulsions, evictions, grand displays of curds and whey, of weights unbidden, and the making thoroughly hollow.

APIS, CATHARTES, LARIDAE, HOLOTHURIAN, PROSTREMA ULTIMA

Below is sawdust, soil span, I spread it thick but trim. Before you is the emetic dawn. Behind you is the ipecac night. Above you is a lintel and the pressure of a head too high.

And by such sign, this is read:

what is meant for the earth cannot be held in air,
what is meant for the body is meant for neither

The Timeless Art of Regurgitation

I'm sorry about your Cardigan,
I suppose my acid-added wrinkle
 couldn't be quelled
and maybe I've been cleaning my ears
too much but could you repeat
your answer?

Not because I don't believe you—
for I have always believed in a thing
like you— more so that you know for sure
        what to do with all this upchuck

Or should I be shutting up about now,
like a soldier, about-face, and never
        bother you
with tender questions again? Because
        the way I feel

north of this pylorus, caudal to this tongue—
because if you said *no*, then this is an act
        of lightness, a reaching
or retreating, like a vulture with its spew.

In which case, would you hold my jacket
as well? Would you repeat it to my beak,
        while I run off to carry on
like carrion, undistinguished in the road?

And if *yes,* then I must be making
sure, like a Coney Island gull,
offering what I've eaten rather than
face that soft consumption
spooling in your teeth.

Take these boardwalk curds
instead of my piteous pounds, and
        if it doesn't suit
you, answer again and I'll come up
with something better. It's my Birthday
and there's cake down here somewhere.

Scarecrow in a Tuxedo

and not just a tux t-shirt but the real thing,
dry-cleaned reminder that the clearest
plan for standing is to stand, the truest
route for sitting is to keep standing, and
to do *that* you must wear a thing that can
never know crease.

You ever see a scarecrow with a cane?
They spout their anger at Kachinas smoking
dope beside their lawn. They conduct
themselves like a Philharmonic, full of crash
and brisk endowment, votive measures
shot to shit.

The best gala guests are those with no fingers
for the finger foods, no chutes for squall
Champagne. They add shape to swole surrounds,
like teabags crimped for sucking, once too steep,
now eager to ride the banister, petticoat and all.
Held up to—what?

Never a living body left to mend, we viciously
cater, valet with the best pressed plackets
while coke goes flaming like dragons up
their caves. And nevermind the birds whose
murders justify the bill. But does it ride up?
Wedgy in the straw.

Turkey in the hay—they say they don't know
the meaning of the song. Yet, when I survey
the ballroom all I see are stuffed shirts working
hard at hiding their post holes and crossbeams,
and say, it's a lot like Christ, if he was wrong,
or just ashamed.

Not that the two ever comply in company
like this. I'm not reaching for a hot take,
because, hell it'd be an awful shame if this
place went up. Special choice in second-hand
smoke, like, hey if I don't choke on it, no one
would, not here. Not now.

Adjustments and other Insomniads

"Except that," she said, because
we're always in each other's heads,
"they're failing forward, the act of testing
is like hell finding portal in your liver."

          "I wouldn't know," I said, not wanting to
          exit out the back so late at night. "But I can
          sleep on the pull-out. I don't think it will be
          ironic if we refuse to treat it as such."

And outside, I could hear someone
muting an argument with a trashcan lid,
like so many band members marching
down an alley for a light, or a puff of
something righteous, but oh, I wouldn't
be doing anything about it, I was trying
too hard at the time to prove I wasn't
worth the awkward blocks of text

          "But what I do know," I said, because,
          hell, I'm always saying something.
          "Is that sleep is just a special mental
          indifference, something we need with
          out expressly knowing why."

"It's filthy in here," she said, and it
was indeed filthy. "And if you're so
terrified of the way out, let me help
you invest in the ways back in."

          And we were needed despite the filth,
          despite the fifth sound against the door
          calling all the tenets to clusterfucks beneath.
          I became the heaviest head between us,
          and she fell backwards like a tourist
          spanning wind, and woe to the ants
          who saw us then, their empire like interior
          Gomorrah full of passionate spleen.

"It doesn't have to be an accident,"
she said, so full of dim divide, like
trouble growling over a lid. "Sighing
over wide alleys to prove you can
still breathe, but I can't dream as well
as you. For me, it is the echo that
speaks. I am only its omen."

And your name is?

I am much less likely
to spill my coffee if I drink it nude.
And thus I must suffer
stains or loneliness—stains or—
       is it all the same? No, I should
think not, because wearing ruddy
       Rorschach is company enough,
dependency enough, descendingly—
       enough! I need not qualify
my clothish blotch of friends.
       Rather I'd wish upon a day
too spouted when freakish drops
       splatter into form. When I might
stop along a crosswalk, all my porous
       faces raised, and ponder:
what is this that brings black rain,
       but is no cloud?
The sky as clear as witching
       bleed of woad. Oh God—
is this what it is to mature?
       I mean, friends are like
volcanic glass, in that, I know how
       they are made, but that
doesn't mean I know how
       to make them.

Experimental Salvo No. 1

Absolutely no
squirrel this time!
Get 'em while

Hot Dogs! Fre
sh, hot, Hot Dogs!
100% real beef!

there still Hot
Dogs! Limited ti
me offer! Buy

Hot Dogs! Get
your Hot Dogs
here! Hot Dogs!

    o
 on   g
   e   et
ne   fr e e !
H   ot D o g s !
N o w w ith ext ra
    n it ra t e s!

Sweat, Needles

The damn dirt isn't even the worst of it

a thought of three years
with pine needles stuck to my skin
nature's favor weaponized

I have half a mind
to say that I don't care
but that other half does
somewhere, however,

when I talk about where
I lost my skin I talk about
a bench (or was it a bleacher?)
and a fence beside it
where a girl (or a bully) chased me
into the matte pine

I'm only happy
with the story when I talk about it
and I don't talk about it

I just write about it
and you're right, that's not the same
as talking

That's the Eden ease of it—
a complete reprise of the dream
where you shower
                 pull it down
        not now,
                go,
                  get ready for bed

Out of the Keys

A child was screaming on my flight.
I was going home to attend a funeral
                    for a pinball machine.

So, I gave the kid my Amazon Fire
hoping he'd like the way its little boxes
scroll sidelike
                    first slow, in cold butter modum
                    then fast, like duck yolk cut
                            over thawed bread

                    and he liked it so much
                    he smashed its glass
                    with his nose.

Now you might be thinking
that child is a dick, or that I'm a dick
for giving a child something made of glass.

But
            I'm here to tell you that we all
                    have it coming

What with the ways we scratch,
            and hurt each other's laps

What with all the upstream havoc,
            and our habit of patting our pockets
            like wooly little aphids
            waving at each other
            to slow down, stop,
            go back the way you came

The Autotomist

I have never needed a tail
(would you have wanted me so clean?)
but I have worn, in certain lapses,
another head wagging from my rear,
the *double en passant* entirely me and yet,
        as one who sees the world
        upside down, *he* speaks
        in all things contrary
              and yet, I'd find it fine
              to live lizardly
              and sunned.

Call me skink, and I shall call you
friend, but my extra head will roll you
rudely up into some joint of names,
suck you down to smolder, chew the roach.

Ask me which mouth makes our music
and I will sing you every humor of whiskey,
while *he* croups *his* damaged pedantry
and shrapnels you with phlegm.

        I could lick my
        eye if it meant
        I might keep staring,
      do so much with such little
      arms, whose scuttle I cannot
      fathom within the limits of my lank.
By then I'm sure you'll have had enough.
And I should tell you now, *he* won't have voice
or limbless vigor to swear *his* salmonella
after I've pinched *him* off. After I'm gone.
      Hold *him* over your proper head,
      breathe where *he* had breath, recall

again how very real *he* once looked—
　　　　there are many
　　　　ways to survive you.
　　　　This is my favorite one.

The Kakuurpuura

The Kakuurpuura possesses a chitinous shell
to protect the pristine slumgullion inside its serrations.
Radial glochidia make for miraculous munitions,
and, when swallowed whole, a Kakuurpuura explodes
its needlings, its pardoned intrusions, suffered arteries,
blending breach-teeth, bony gnasheries all up inside
a hungry motherfucker. A curious evolution, sure,
but a reminder that even genes understand
        the potency of spite.

Never in the history of calm down

has the calming down calmed down
has someone come home reeking of light litter,
their pockets akimbo-paunched with jazz

in the vinyl room
        smoke goes like
                savory kindle and heel
                        like Ipanema and halitose serene

Never in the history of stand up
has the standing up stood up
has surrendered gesture truly given up the game
piano twins twenty paces in exchange

in the tarot street
        sigh smooths like
                braille cobble and throne
                        like Imperator and Fool inverse

Never in the history of hold me
has the holding me held me
has what I am conformed with what others enclosed
appending fish swimming in different pelagic zones

in the concrete hangnail
        steam clings like
                brick shed and paraffin
                        like erasure and too, too soft

Writing

it is as easy as lying, or playing the pipe,
it's tight thunder passing one sound for another,
only sourcing sweetness with its proper stops

I would play on myself, I would govern these
interruptions and delude the growth until each note
shrills higher than any human hearing can bear

I might fall into deft sense or dreaming furrow,
know each time of day as doubtless as any
blind man in a glass room full of sun

and when I find my assurance, I will not need words,
because the indulgence of one is the atrophy
of the other, a submission no one can ever truly read

there's no shame in the divide, but I wrote a letter
to the Editor anyway and asked when I should expect
his rejection and the next day my cat died

as if life hasn't lived since Bobbie Hooke first
gazed into the cloister maze of scum, the cells
becoming quanta, quickly forgetting what is meant

and what it means to seem akin, I have two hands
but I can't stress their function, so I turn into mosquito,
sending pioneering protozoa directly to your brain

and maybe when I'm happy I won't have to keep
making these mirrored things, inside, I find myself
one shore away from the error of my Atlantic

outside, I am trying to think of a word that rhymes
with espresso, and all the while, beneath the beam,
the mystery is betrayed, colors cut, cells are dying

The Urolith

Lithotripsy

a joke

A fool comes to his local apothecary and asks him to brew a special draught.

"Let us dispense with beauty for a moment, as beauty is no pure standard by which to derive appreciation."

"Huh?" says the apothecary, as he is hard of hearing.

"What of works that disgust, or thrill, or frighten? What of the ape that sees worms in his fruit for the first time? The fish overcome with relief when it falls from the angler's stern? What of a rock that inclines toward earth and earth toward celestia?"

"Huh?" the apothecary says again because he is also a very confused man.

"Make it a draught of access. Poultice up whatever screwball stents you've got a'clanging in that dimple you call a shelf. Make it part blue and part red. Make it threnody with niftiness, distill it with ill-intent but conjunct it with rough pleasure. Tamp it, tap it, wax, and wrap it."

And the apothecary begins preparing something—not quite what the fool asked for, but something whose complexity satisfies the onlooker.

"Is this what you wanted?" the apothecary asks.

The fool takes his bottle in hand. Turns it over, watches how its humor capers. Some weight makes him clutch at his insides. He sits.

"Yes, almost," the fool says. "Like this, but for everyone."

a perpetual letter to my kidney stone

Thank you (worry about what's coming)
for bringing me another pill, thank you for
the tilt and curl, when I crouch in the clinic,
so that only my hand is visible, clawed on the desk.
        When I say I have *a little problem*,
        I mean you,   my seven millimeters
        reigning rough in renal causeway

I walked crooked for a day,   concerned
my already worry-swollen students,   blushed
a friend's porcelain to rustier shade,   called
impediment into group therapy,   and
reminded myself to scream as clots
came mucking out my smallest   end

and yeah, I suppose it'd be nice
to live a life of unobstruction
but there's also laughing with your doctor
as they try to explain how to strain your own urine
        and, honestly, that's wild—
        it sure beats having
        nothing to complain about

an alternative to stethoscopes

You know, the funny thing about Marvin Gaye is that, after he was shot by his father, nothing really changed in the world. Which is a terribly bleak thing to think about, but I find myself thinking about it a lot these days. And I suppose it's not funny unless I make it so, and if I can't laugh at something so perfectly horrible, then what good is laughter anyway? You might as well give me a foot long needle with a flag at one end. "You plunge it into your heart," they say, "if it moves then we will know you were alive."

----

a poem in which I stick up for Ea-Nasir

Let's face it,   Nanni is a difficult man.
So are we all, all difficult then,
but does this   mean we smelt ourselves
in sconce-ill   indignations? Do we
lacquer into   some slant harass?
Do we hold   out rough stones,
call it ore,   and cry to that heaven
        over heaven?

I took time   out of the future
to learn this, to cut with wedge,
cuneiform   all up one side of brick,
and you of   all people turn my eye
to dust, you   who Guinness holds
as oldest in   critique. Contempt, like any
stimulating   brew, is sweetest in the bottom
        of the cup.

I wonder   what complaints of me
will live in   three thousand years.
The slights   like demons sniffing in your
windows.   Another poet hanging her
totem in   ward of what I wrote.
In boredom,   if not in actual apotrope.
My words   are ingots. Take them if you
        would take them.

Or do not   if you find them inferior.
I would   cheat you otherwise. I would
keep each   platelet hour hostage in my
sacks. On   all sides, many ruthless spears.
So when I   stand here in your yard,
choking   smoked refinement, do not
belittle me.   Someday, I hope to be as
        tired as you.

Burn me out

Lose me if you love me, let the lantern hit the floor,
let the sparking of its falling spread its flames across the door,
Fill the fallowness of focus which comes blustered with a shriek
from the hollow of the sinus where your heart has grown too weak.
Take a lungful of my smoking, prickled light with cinders' swirl
burn me out of your sclera, harry all your hairs to curl.
Let skin succumb to crackle, and let it caramelize the glaze
of my sweet and simple succor singeing quick within the blaze.
Marvel at the swift succession of your hearth replacing home
turning thatch to ashen atrophy and then all to catacomb.
All becoming thus untethered toward that warming snow of worth
that coats the blackened drywall with the pungent palls of earth.

And to say that I'm a fire is to only speak the facts,
while to say the heart's a muscle is to say that it contracts
and extends itself indefinite, impossible to contain
save all the awful falling waters intervening from the brain.
I think we're more than our assurances, insured for incidentals,
more than eerie little ecstasies sprung bright from elementals.
So thank God for salt and ceremony, thank Hell for what retains,
every powdered heap between us fallen from our white cremains,
this Pyrrhic trance and prophecy which so benevolently becalms
these anguished simulations of warmth between our palms.

Because any mete of friction is anesthetic to the skin,
a third-degree reminder which left the leaden linens thin,
our shawls too charred apart from us in this rigor mortal braid
some tactful black reminder of concessions that we made.
But of all the fats that made us, that have had their time to rend
so little's left to suggest that they were not made to end.
And yes, fire's a tired metaphor, I guess I've yet to learn
not every line that I've made rhyme was also made to burn.

Protozoan

O manxome molts
in protozoan slumber
which flail the flagella,
gorge the Golgi, repose
in halting hibernation.

but an amoeba cannot sleep—
it has no brain.
however, this is poetry
so bear with me. pretend.
it's fun to speculate
about single-celled dreams.

do ciliates scintillate?
do plasmodia plod?
do they skirt the ebb
endogenous,
edge their nights
with empty elan?

or do they wonder
        about choice?

do they dream
of shoes,
        & socks,
                & feet?

Good, Without Qualifications

Will I will
        this sconce of seem
    dark in thought
    but bright in dream?

Will I will
        and like a fly
    will to love this
    will to die?

Will I will
        but take no heart
    in all the willingness
    apart?

Will I will
        and will it good?
    Would I can
    if well I should?

There are no beautiful words for canal

I suppose it could be *nahar* in Hindi,
or *unga* in Japanese. And I don't mind
the numerous *gesundheits* that follow
my mentions of *shaduf*, so long as
it remains known how pierced and fairly
perilous the sun rode down from his
   daily boat in the land of Egypt,
   full of galloping wither
     and decadent
     lash.

And like a sound which never prospers,
and soil, scar-baked from either side,
we slake the scathing need in one, and
in another bygone bed, in a house of stone,
in a heaven of stone, and in wood, and in
steel, and in glass, and in stone again,
   we drank everything
   and sang everything
     and said nearly
     everything

in every tongue, with every shape
sated human mouths can make, and
some without breath, who dug our
irrigation and died retracted in fading
gloam, extinguished with the tyrant sun.
Camlas, siki, terusan—like fleeing mites
   from mouths, names
   ill with ambient
     drift and moisture
     retracing.

Algea

Who is Pain

I might have pleasured freely, though I really can't be sure.
But what's to say of deft dismay to the defter epicure?
They round themselves entirely, til pleasures there accrete
in stony inefficiencies that block your wetted meat.
Only then the shock will crump your step, and possum-tilt your spine
with omens strung *de novo* in your torso's intertwine.
Don't believe me? Just you wait, my tonic swirls the flood,
and inserts intermittent stops and emissive clots of blood.
The burning nerve shall set you safe, too contented is the stain
that better marks the puncture, than the shapeless bale of sprain.
Shave me all the sparser then, diagnose me to my face,
name me as *Causalgia* and I will wrack you stiff in place.
You can't look up, you can't look down, *here* you will behave
drought yourself of sorrows and other excuses that you crave.

It's Thursday

and I am overcome,
which is not what Thursdays are designed
       to do. So where do I complain
       if not in a poem, that no one will read
       unless I force them to?

I cannot shake
(except that I do) on mornings when I wake
       before I'm needed, and needed
       when I shouldn't still stir. Yesterday,
       I found a burned spoon.

People don't think
I live in a strapped neighborhood but then,
       sometimes, I point my laptop's camera
       through the slit blinds where
       siren lights glaze busted doors.

Those same blinds
won't keep out the sun, so I toss, slip dead
       another hour and suffer a dream
       where, this time, we come so close
       to fucking it aches.

I don't recognize
her high-rise apartment, but I tell myself
       (again) that I'm over it, that we
       hate each other anyway and that
       it's healthy to know.

But just before
I really regret my dreaming, a car door shuts,
       bed wraps shed, I look out, sliced thin,
       a man holds another against a wall.
       I wish them well. A siren.

The Poet comes to Capitol

The gates groaned hello when I arrived,
my arms overbrimming, feet sanded
down, and a trail of poems swirling
like leaf litter on the river-rutted road
behind.

And the consul was a mean-looking
motherfucker with a goatee and a pack
of cigarettes in his sleeve. But he spoke
with all the gravity of a well, and told me:
sit, like a dog.

He had them take the haystack
of papers from my arms, drank whiskey
with a straw, and asked me if I could
be anyone I wanted, and I, husked with thirst,
said *yes*.

Everyone laughed. He grunted a command
and then someone poured a cup of Valvoline
on my head, gave me a wreath of pillow
stuffing, and dragged me, shaking,
to the gate.

That'll teach you to bring your words,
the consul scorned, *though I expect you are godly
and of moral mien. Please, try to see it our way,
we've got a real good thing going here and we try
not to think about it.*

I Discard the Image of My Waking from Anesthesia

a post-surgery agitation

Water has its inclinations, earth too, its inclinations.
If I contain a stone, it must incline to be inside of me.
If I spill water, does it not incline to be entwined with earth?
Blood, too, like the fire desiring its heaven, pleads to meet
                the molten core.

When I wake, they tell me everything went well, the surgeons
acted according to every rule, my channels, my body yielded
to every scope and tucked me ever reckless into a loafish bolt of cloth.
Fabric too, has its inclinations, even in its fray, even if no strings
                could be teased out.

Later, when I shower, water inclines itself toward a hairy drain,
implies it's needed leaving like porcelain desires to be dry.
I see what hangs off and out of me, wicking and sticking itself
to skin, freckle and flex, crinkles and lumped out fissures
                from greener stoop.

Soundly, I'm enclyning to a kindly sort of stede, this tenuous
need toward another state. These days, we use a language
of submission: gravity is obeyed, biology is fulfilled, systems in intimate
impress, exclusion and illusions of cases becoming laws, of senses
                accused of too much wit.

The tube they left inside me, now removed, watches
from my wastebasket all smug, like it's solved some moral
puzzle, as if to say, "I've acted against my inclinations,
I've uprooted myself, the rest, you say, is not wanting
                the whip, the leaden heels."

That first night, I take my oxycodone and remember that addicts
also have their inclinations. Clerics, their inclinations. Dam builders,
inclinations. All have their ways of staying dead. I keep my head

down when I pass the preacher, the gadabout evangelists with their
foam-core signs.

"What is God?" one asks, the others plunging pocket knives
into tuna cans, the fish once inclined to salt, the salt to sea.
I recall the tinny taste from a sandwich my mother made me. I don't
answer because saying anything is to forget the meaning of the thing
one says.

Although I am inclined toward heights, and keeling over bedpans,
and panicked cords of seam. Although, when I emerged from the gas
I finished my previous thought: I made a stone, and what I make
hurts me sometimes. Despite the inclinations. Despite the head risen
out of Horeb.

What is God?
Not   me.

Appendix
The Somatoliths

Gastrolith

~~Bezoar~~

~~Coprolite~~

~~Enterolith~~

Regurgitalith

~~Cololiths~~

~~Bromolith~~

~~Otolith~~

Bufonite

~~Snakestone~~

~~Coccolithophore~~

~~Tonsillolith~~

Urolith

~~Cholelith~~

~~Rhinolith~~

~~Phlebolith~~

~~Omphalolith~~

Acknowledgments

"Pectoralis Major" and "The Post-oneiric Breakfast Debacle" were first published in November of 2022 by *The Rumen Literary Journal*

"Urodela" was first published in *The Talon Review*

"The timeless art of regurgitation" was first published in Poetica Review

"A lonely hotel courtyard in the middle of Atlanta" was first published by *Book of Matches*

"The Loiter You Do" was first published in *The Artemis Journal*

"Writing" was first published by *Quiver Review*

"Burn me out" was first published by *Carolina Muse*

About the Author

James Cole is a poet, author, filmmaker, and neuroscientist based out of Morgantown, WV.

Born in Roanoke, VA, James went on to study creative writing, medieval-renaissance studies, and neuroscience at The College of William and Mary. In 2023, James earned his Ph.D. in neuroscience from the University of Virginia, where he studied neural development and retinal degenerative diseases. He currently teaches neuroscience and psychology as an Assistant Professor at West Virginia University.

James' writings have appeared in numerous publications over the years, including Poetica Review, Oddball Magazine, Carolina Muse, among others. His first collection, *Crow, come home*, was published in 2019 through VerbalEyze Press. Aside from his publishing, James was the founder of the Charlottesville Poetry Critique Circle, an instructor at WriterHouse, a Board of Governors Member for the Virginia Writers Club, and a judge for the Virginia Poetry Out Loud competition. He has collaborated with many artists and performers over the years, including the Eunoia Creative Arts Community, The Bridge Progressive Arts Initiative, and Visible Records Gallery. From 2022 to 2023 he hosted the Poetry Live! Showcase in collaboration with Live Arts Theater. In 2022, he co-founded The Rumen Literary Arts Journal and continues to serve as chief editor for poetry and co-editor for fiction and non-fiction.

Beyond the literary sphere, James is a fan of all things ancient and arcane. He is a practitioner of historic European martial arts and a former sport fencer. James enjoys board games, trivia, and cooking.

More of his work can be found at jamescoleauthor.com

Also check out The Rumen at therumen.com

www.ingramcontent.com/pod-product-compliance
Lightning Source LLC
Chambersburg PA
CBHW051331120626
46547CB00016B/2495